LIVING IN
EUROPE

David Flint

Wayland

EUROPE

Editors: Janet De Saulles and Deb Elliott
Series Design: Bridgewater Design
Book Design: Jackie Berry

First published in 1992 by Wayland (Publishers) Ltd.,
61 Western Road, Hove, BN3 1JD, England

British Library Cataloguing in Publication Data

Flint, David
    Living in Europe. – (Europe Series)
    I. Title II. Series
    940

ISBN 0 7502 0335 8

Typeset by Dorchester Typesetting Group Ltd.
Printed in Italy by G. Canale C.S.p.A., Turin
Bound in France by A.G.M.

ACKNOWLEDGEMENTS

Associated Press/Topham 41; J. Allan Cash Ltd. 14, 19, 20, 21, 24 (top);
Cephas (Stuart Boreham) 28, (Mick Rock) 43; Chapel Studios 24 (bottom);
Eye Ubiquitous Frontispiece, (Mike Feeney) 17, 40; G. S. F. Picture Library
11; Hutchison Library 5 (Nancy Durrell McKenna), 10, 16, 27, 44; Oskar
Radelli 7, 22, 30; Tony Stone Worldwide (Tom Raymond) 4, (Joe Cornish) 8,
(Stephen Johnson) 12, (Colin Prior) 23, (David H. Endersbee) 26, (Mike King)
31, (Francois Puyplat) 27 (top), (Charlie Waite) 38; Wayland Picture Library
15; Zefa 9, 13, 18, 25, 31, 37 (bottom). All artwork is by Malcolm Walker.

Contents

Europe's people

Europe currently has a large population. This, however, has not always been the case. In the last 200 years most European countries have gone from having relatively few people to having many. These changes have been called the population cycle, which has four stages.

At stage one countries have a high birth-rate (measured as the number of babies born each year for each 1,000 people) and a high death-rate (measured as the number of deaths each year for each 1,000 people). At this stage the population is only increasing slowly, as was typical of Britain in

Better health care for the elderly has radically improved life expectancy in many countries.

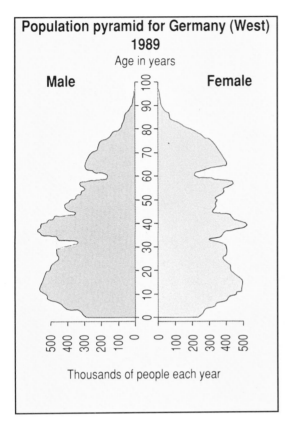

Population pyramid for Germany (West) 1989

Age in years

Male   Female

Thousands of people each year

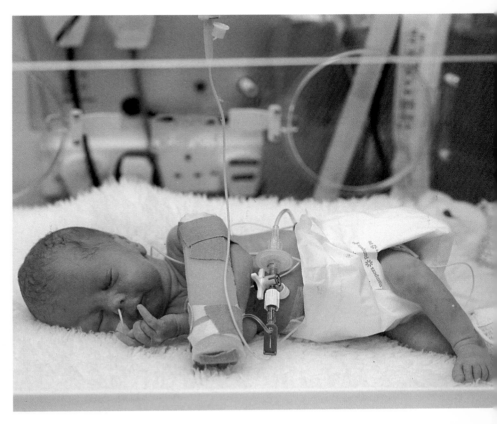

the eighteenth century and Russia in the nineteenth century.

At stage two the death-rate declines as a result of medical advances, such as better hygiene, sanitation and disease prevention. However, the birth-rate stays high, so there is rapid population growth. This happened in Britain, France and Germany in the nineteenth century, and then Greece and Russia in the twentieth century.

At stage three there is a continued fall in the death-rate as new medical advances are made. The birth-rate also begins to fall,

so population growth slows down. This happens when people decide to have fewer children, usually because they want a higher standard of living. Falling population growth occurred in Britain, Norway, Sweden, France, Germany and Italy in the early twentieth century and, more recently, in Greece and Spain.

By stage four of the population cycle, both birth-rates and death-rates are low, so population growth is also very slow. In some cases the population size may start to decline, as happened in France in the 1970s.

Above **Modern fertility drugs frequently lead to multiple births. This premature baby, one of triplets, is being closely monitored in a high-tech intensive care unit.**

Above left **Germany's population pyramid shows a common pattern. Births are diminishing and the number of elderly people is growing.**

Opposite page **Governments are building more schools.**

Below **The countries of Europe.**

The result of these population changes can best be seen in a population pyramid. This divides the population into age groups, with the percentage of females on the right and males on the left of the central axis. Many countries, such as Germany, have a narrow 'base' to the population pyramid. This is a sign of a low birth-rate, but it also shows the increasing numbers of older people. This has

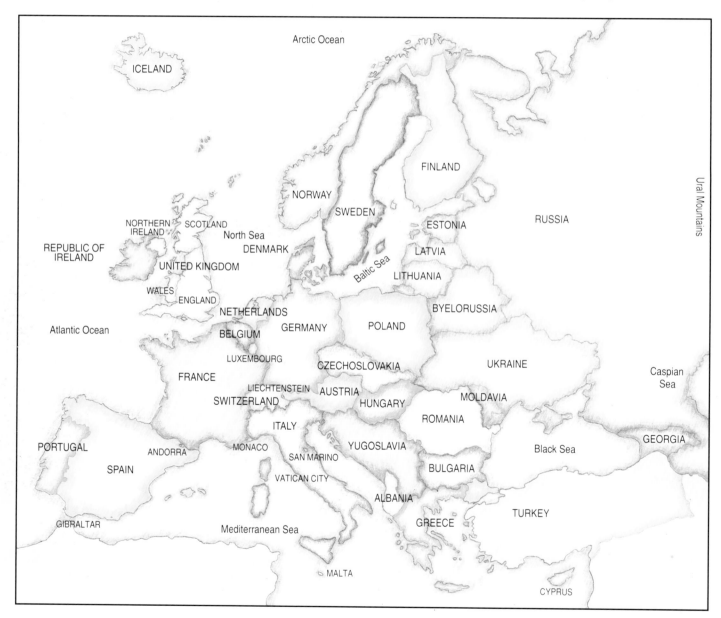

important implications for planning the country's future. It may be necessary, for example, to build more hospitals and clinics and train more doctors to cope with the needs of a growing number of old people.

Empty places, crowded places

The people of Europe are not spread evenly over the Continent. Some places are very crowded, others are quite empty, as the map on page 6 shows.

We can find out why there are so few people in the empty areas by looking at basic geographical and climatic factors:

- Some areas, such as the Pyrenees or the Alps, are too high and too steep for farming. This makes it very difficult for people living there to earn money.
- Some places are too cold all year round to allow crops to grow. This means that areas such as northern Sweden or northern Russia can only support very few people.
- Drought is a problem in parts of Europe such as central Spain. Here, if there are no rivers to provide water for irrigation, farming may be difficult or impossible.
- Some areas of Europe, such as northern Norway or Iceland, lack economic resources such as coal, oil or minerals so these countries can support few people.

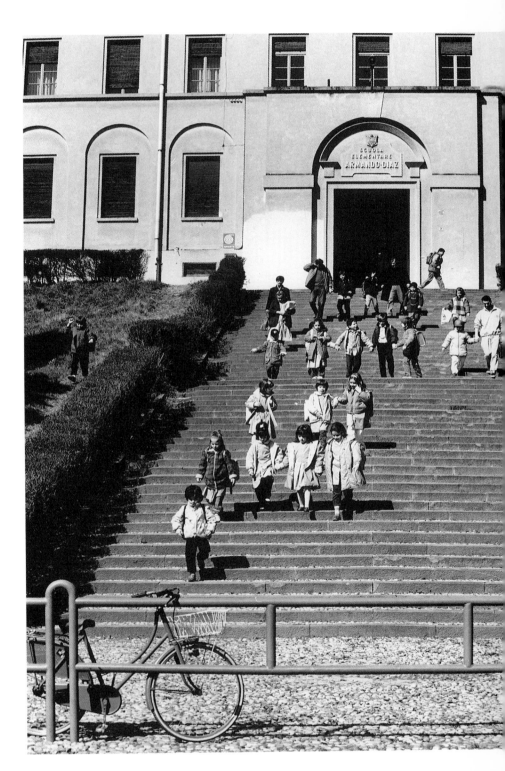

● Other parts of Europe, such as northern Greece or the western part of Iceland, are a long way from the capital city or other main centres of industry.

Other areas are crowded. This might be the case because of the following reasons:

● Places which have a warm climate and enough rainfall to allow a wide range of farming practices often have a large population. Northern France, the Netherlands, central Germany and the Ukraine fall into this particular category.

The Apennine Mountain region of central Italy has varied landscapes and fertile soils. Farming in the area supports large rural populations.

The Côte d'Azur, in southern France, has been a tourist centre for many decades. The palm-fringed Promenade des Anglais, in Nice, is a popular attraction.

- Areas with rich, deep soils are also good for farming and so attract people. The valley of the river Po in Italy is one example.
- Popular holiday areas must have large numbers of local people to cater for the needs of the tourists. Parts of south-west Spain, southern France and Italy are examples of extremely crowded tourist areas.
- Places rich in economic resources such as coal, oil or minerals often become important centres of industry. For example, the Ruhr area of Germany or the Donets area of the Ukraine are extremely crowded industrial centres.
- Capital cities such as Paris, London, Rome, Dublin, Madrid and Athens attract many people The areas around these capitals are also densely populated.

This high-rise housing block in Moscow is situated adjacent to the noise and pollution of the city's power stations.

● Important cities which are centres of commerce, administration and education are other crowded places. Marseilles, Hamburg and Kiev are examples.

People on the move

Within Europe lots of people are moving from place to place. There are many different kinds of movement:–

● **Daily movement**, such as journeys into a city to work then back home again.

● **Seasonal movement**, such as a holiday outing for one, two or more weeks.

● **Temporary movement**, for example when people move away from home to find work for a few months, then return home.

● **Permanent movement**, such as migration, when people leave one place, like a crowded town, for the peace and quiet of the countryside.

Both temporary and permanent moves are particularly important in Europe. For example, lots of

people in Turkey go to find temporary jobs in Germany, Switzerland and other rich countries as guest workers (see pages 14-15). Permanent movement is usually of two types:
1. Leaving the countryside, in countries such as Russia, Greece and Italy, to live in cities.
2. Leaving cities, such as London, Berlin, or Madrid, and going to live in villages in the countryside.

Why do people move? What makes them leave an area they know to go to a new area, often far away? They decide to move in response to a combination of factors. 'Push' factors encourage them to leave a particular area, and 'pull' factors attract them to a different place.
'Push' factors include:
● A lack of jobs, which forces people to move in order to find work. This is happening in rural parts of Greece and Russia.
● Problems of living in big cities. These include pollution, noise, crime and the high cost of housing and transport. In cities such as Paris, London and Rotterdam, people are leaving town for a better quality of life in the countryside.

Big cities can provide better services, such as nursery schools or hospitals, than rural areas.

Left **Sophisticated facilities, such as this indoor shopping centre, can attract people to large cities.**

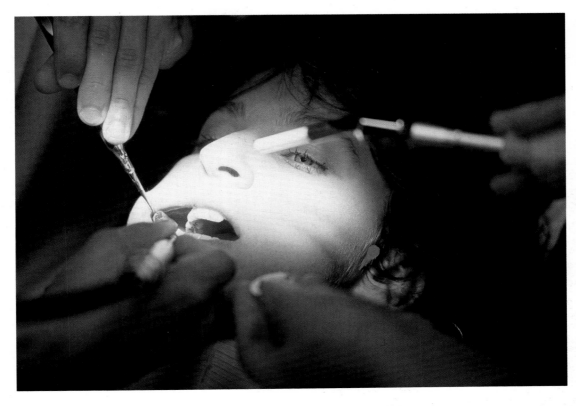

Right **The availability of a high standard of health care is often a factor which draws people to cities.**

- A lack of services, such as schools, hospitals and libraries. In rural parts of Portugal and Sweden this is encouraging people to move to towns.
- Serious problems such as starvation and war. At the end of the Second World War in 1945, millions of German-speaking people migrated from Poland to Germany. They wanted to live among people with the same language and customs.

'Pull' factors include:

- The appeal of a better paid job, or simply any job at all. This has encouraged people from Ireland to seek work in England, and people from Italy to seek work in Switzerland.
- The hope of better housing. In rural parts of Portugal and Greece houses often have no electricity, running water or other services. People go to the towns in search of better houses and flats.
- The attraction of more and better services. In Russia people are leaving the countryside because they want the better shops, schools, hospitals, libraries and entertainment facilities available in many of the larger towns such as Moscow.

Below left There are many Turkish guest workers in West Germany. They frequently do dangerous or unskilled jobs which are not wanted by the local population.

Below right This pie-chart shows the countries of origin of Germany's guest workers. Turkish workers form the substantial majority.

● The idea of a better quality of life. Many people in Germany, the Netherlands and Britain have moved away from towns. This is because they feel it will be better to bring up their children in the countryside, where they believe there is less pollution, crime, noise and vandalism.

Guest workers

Guest workers are people who leave their home country in order to find a job in one of the richer European countries, such as Germany, France and Switzerland. Most of Europe's guest workers come from Turkey, Yugoslavia or North Africa, as the diagrams show. Often just one person in a family leaves home to work abroad

as a guest worker. After a few years, if he or she is successful, other members of the family will come to join them.

During times of economic growth, for example in the 1960s, there were many jobs in the richer countries like Germany. A lot of people in the richer countries did not want to do the dirtier, unskilled and often dangerous jobs, such as refuse disposal. So there were plenty of jobs and not enough people to do them. At this stage the guest workers were made welcome. They did not object to doing less attractive work because they could earn a living. There are now about 7.5 million guest workers in Europe, with another 8 million dependants.

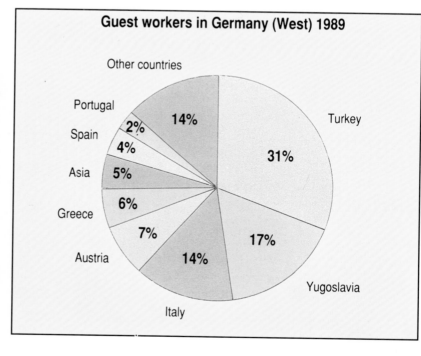

Guest workers in Germany (West) 1989

Other countries
Portugal
Spain
Asia
Greece
Austria
Italy
Turkey
Yugoslavia

14%
2%
4%
5%
6%
7%
14%
31%
17%

Today economic growth has slowed down in the richer countries and many people have lost their jobs. These unemployed people can resent foreign guest workers because they feel that they are stealing their jobs. This is a particular problem in Germany now that reunification has taken place. As the populations of East and West Germany have combined, unemployment has risen sharply.

Guest workers often live in and around big cities. They retain their own language, culture and religion and generally lead a different lifestyle from that of the local people. This has created social tensions in some places. High concentrations of guest workers can result in local people feeling outnumbered. For example, 70 per cent of all pupils in Frankfurt schools come from guest worker families.

Some problems that guest workers face

Life is not easy for guest workers for a number of reasons. Many cannot afford the fares to visit relatives in their home countries. Feelings of homesickness are common. Guest workers are sometimes made to feel unwelcome by local people, who resent the presence of another culture. Demonstrations against guest workers can lead to violence, and there are programmes to

persuade some guest workers to return home.

Guest workers also face a lack of good housing. They often have to live in overcrowded slums which lack sanitation and are insect-infested. In France some foreign workers live in shanty towns called *bidonvilles*, where houses are made of scraps of wood, old petrol cans, plastic or any other materials people can find.

Some guest workers have poor diets and little access to medical services and so their children may suffer from illness.

Many of Portugal's guest workers come from its former African colony, Mozambique.

The European lifestyle

Across Europe people live in many different types of housing. Because of the rebuilding that has taken place in most cities, especially since 1945, a lot of people live in modern homes. This modern housing is often the result of urban rebuilding programmes, which aim to knock down old, sub-standard housing, and replace it with modern homes. In the process of modernization, additional facilities such as gardens, play areas, water, electricity and sewage services are all incorporated by the planners.

As a result, many of the up-to-date housing developments in countries as far apart as Sweden, the Netherlands and Spain can look very similar. In an effort to make maximum use of limited space, developers build blocks of flats. Estates consisting of such blocks can rehouse many people but rarely offer examples of attractive, original architecture.

Blocks of residential flats in Naples relieve some of the city's chronic overcrowding.

This farmhouse, with a steep-sided wooden gable, is typical of Dutch rural architecture.

Traditional European houses tend to be much more varied in their style and in the building materials used. They often reflect the area's climate and the local raw materials suitable for house building. For example, traditional Swiss chalets were built of local wood, and the steep overhanging roofs were designed to get rid of heavy winter snowfalls. By contrast, in Mediterranean areas houses tend to be built of local stone, with thick walls and few windows in order to keep the rooms cool in the summer heat.

Many houses in these areas are often painted white to reflect the sunlight. The flat roofs are also put to good use, for drying produce such as grapes.

The second homes issue

In Sweden, Germany, Switzerland and France, many urban families have a second home which is usually in the countryside. This second home is used at weekends and on holidays, for about ninety days each year, to get away from the stresses of living in town.

Most second homes are near the coast or lakes, or in areas of attractive countryside such as mountains. They also have to be within easy reach if their owners are to keep travelling times as short as possible. This means second homes tend to be in villages close to motorways or

Mykonos in Greece is a Mediterranean harbour town. Its flat-roofed, white houses are a cool refuge from the heat of the Mediterranean summers.

main roads. In south Germany many families have second homes in Switzerland and Austria, countries which are only a short drive away on the motorways (Autobahnen). An additional advantage is that the local Swiss or Austrian people also speak the German language.

The number of second homes has increased rapidly during the last ten years. For example in Britain in 1970 there were 170,000 second homes, but now there are 380,000 – more than double the number. Similarly, in the richer European countries, especially Germany, the Netherlands, Norway, Sweden and Finland, the number of second homes is rising dramatically.

The building of second homes in the countryside can bring both advantages and disadvantages. Local people can sell their land or cottages for a good price, and local shops tend to do well from the visitors. Builders often get extra work renovating older houses and flats. However, house prices do rise and this may mean that local people can no longer afford to buy their own property. There is also great pressure on local services such as water and electricity at popular times, for example during the winter ski season or the summer season. People who have lived in the area all their lives can sometimes find

the newcomers noisy and brash so conflicts can arise. For these reasons, second homes create both winners and losers.

Markets, city centres and hypermarkets

Many European cities still have open-air markets. These are important facilities for shopping. Often goods in these markets are cheaper than in larger shops because the stallholders have lower costs and usually sell direct from farm or factory. Such open-air markets are often held in the centre of small towns like Bruges in Belgium or, in the case of larger cities like Paris, just outside the city centre where land is cheaper.

The turf covering these Icelandic farmhouses provides effective insulation against bitterly cold northern winters.

A rich array of cheeses are on display at the famous Alkmaar cheese market in Holland.

There are also still some specialist markets, such as the cheese market in Alkmaar in the Netherlands or the famous flower market at Singel in Amsterdam.

However, despite the importance of open-air markets, the city shopping centre remains the main shopping area for most European towns and cities. Its main advantage is its accessibility, being at the junction of key roads from the suburbs and surrounding towns and villages.

City centres from Athens, to Berlin, Florence or Oslo share a number of key features such as:

● A large number of shops selling a wide variety of goods.

● Big department stores and multinational supermarkets.

● Special shops selling such items as jewellery, antiques, clothes, furniture or electrical goods. People buy such items less frequently but like to compare prices and merchandise in city centre shops.

● Many banks, building societies, travel agents, hairdressers and cafés.

● Many offices, often above or around the main shopping centre.

In recent years, as traffic congestion has increased, more and more city centres like Munich and Bologna have developed into traffic-free, pedestrian precincts.

Hypermarkets began in France in the 1960s, since when they have spread to most other countries. A hypermarket is a very large shopping centre usually on one level. Hypermarkets have grown up at the edge of large towns and cities, where there is space to surround them with large car parks. They are also close to main roads, so they draw in shoppers from a wide area.

Most hypermarkets have one or two large supermarkets as the main tenants, with ten to twenty smaller specialist shops and services in the same centre. Hypermarkets have become popular because they offer a wide range of goods at competitive prices, at sites where parking is easy. In a few places they are proving strong rivals to the shops of the city centre.

Hypermarkets, situated outside town centres, are easily accessible by car, and often provide extensive car parks.

Life in the countryside

All across Europe the countryside is changing. These changes are fundamental and involve all aspects of life, from earning a living and travelling around to going to hospital. One of the main changes is the number of people living in the countryside. In some places, particularly those close to big cities like Frankfurt, Oslo, London, Paris and Berlin, more and more people are choosing to live in the countryside. However in other places, like western Ireland, the Highlands of Scotland, the Massif Central in France and parts of Russia, people are leaving the countryside in large numbers.

Improving life in the countryside

Once people start to leave the countryside a downward spiral begins and this affects the whole area. Usually young people with families are the first to leave. This means there are fewer people left behind in the countryside to pay for all the services such as schools, hospitals and roads. The countryside in some places, such as the Massif Central or western Ireland, seems full of old people. Such people tend to need *more*, not fewer, services such as hospitals.

It is usually young people who are the first to leave the countryside for the cities. An increasingly elderly population is left behind to look after farms and smallholdings.

As more people leave, schools, shops and hospitals close: it is too expensive to provide such services for a few people living scattered across a wide area. With even fewer shops and services, yet more people are tempted to leave the countryside. The downward spiral continues until the area may become empty.

However, governments have become aware of this problem and have taken steps to stop the outflow of people. This is particularly important in Russia. Here the aim is to persuade people to stay in rural areas by improving the quality of life.

There are major building projects to create more village community centres, with cinemas and theatres, and to build modern houses with central heating and all other conveniences. Roads are repaired, or new ones constructed, to connect remote areas with the rest of the country. In some of the larger villages, technical colleges and secondary schools are being built. This means that children no longer need to go away to towns for secondary schooling. Another improvement is to provide more doctors and medical assistants to tour remote areas and treat people in clinics near their homes. Also,

Areas such as Lannoch Moor in Scotland are inaccessible and remote. The few inhabitants have to travel to local towns for services such as schools and hospitals.

So where do they move to? In general, retired people prefer areas with a mild climate such as the south coast of England, or Languedoc and Provence in France. They look for unspoilt areas of countryside, with few industries or large towns. They also like to live close to the sea.

When retired people move into a rural area, they do not always mix with the local people. This can lead to social tension. Retired people also create an extra demand for local services, such as transport and hospitals. Many retired people buy a house or flat in their new area. This has caused the price of property to rise so that some locals can no longer afford

Left **In Co. Galway, Ireland, new bungalows are gradually replacing derelict cottages in isolated country areas.**

Below **Maidenbower, in Sussex, is a growing commuter village. Many of its residents travel to work in the nearby new town of Crawley or London.**

home-study courses are being provided. These use radio and television to help people continue their education.

Moving into the countryside

In some parts of Europe, people are leaving the towns and moving into the countryside. One group of people making this move is those who have retired from work. At present, in Britain, France, Germany, Norway and Sweden about 10 per cent of people move house when they retire, and the numbers are growing.

The case of Russia

Until recently large numbers of people in Russia lived on farms and in villages in the countryside. In 1961 nearly 61 per cent of all Russian citizens lived in rural areas. But now less than 30 per cent of Russian people live in the countryside. This movement of people away from the countryside is called rural depopulation. People are leaving the countryside for four main reasons:

• Farming on the large, formerly state-owned collective (group-run) farms is becoming more and more mechanized. This means that fewer farm workers are needed.

• In some parts of Russia farming has always been difficult, especially in areas with thin, infertile soils, and steep slopes. Eventually people decide to seek a better life elsewhere.

• There are few job opportunities in many rural areas.

• Housing, education, health and other services are often poorer in the countryside than in the growing towns.

• Large, state-owned farms are being broken up and sold to farmers.

to buy homes in the area.

In parts of Europe, such as south Germany or the eastern Netherlands, villages in the countryside are growing as commuters move in. These newcomers buy their homes in the villages but work in a nearby town or city, such as Munich or Rotterdam. In some countries, such as Britain, Belgium and Germany, people can spend up to four hours each day travelling to and from work, although the average time is now about two hours a day.

Housing in cities is not inevitably better than rural districts. Often houses, like this building in the Old Town of Buchara, Uzbekistan, are old and dilapidated.

Left **Houses in Northern Europe are far more likely to have indoor toilets than in the South.**

Below left **Many modern buildings in town centres, such as this office block, are intended to enhance the urban landscape.**

Right **In overcrowded cities many sporting events take place in the city streets.**

Below **The Old Town, the Muslim quarter in the centre of Samarkand.**

areas of park and grass for their leisure and enjoyment. In the past these green spaces were small or non-existent, except for a few large royal parks like St. James' in London and The Tuileries in Paris.

Sometimes there is a shortage of open space, especially in the industrial towns and conurbations. The Ruhr in Germany is an example of such a conurbation.

New towns

In many parts of Europe, completely new towns have been built to provide an alternative to the problems of overcrowding, congestion and poor housing in older towns and cities. The idea of

Green space in the Ruhr

The Ruhr is one of Europe's most important industrial areas. The basis of this industrial might was coal mining, steel making, engineering and chemicals. Unfortunately, the rapid growth of so much industry left little open space.

It also created serious environmental problems by polluting the air and water, as well as creating derelict mines, disused rivers, railways and canals, together with slag and rubbish heaps. The situation was very serious by 1920, when there were 3,000 people for every kilometre of open space.

Improving the Ruhr's green space

In the 1920s the Ruhr Plan was started, which created a series of riverside walks in the Ruhr valley. A start was also made on removing waste, levelling slag heaps and creating recreation areas. Now there are Green Areas, Area Parks, Leisure Areas, Leisure Zones and Leisure Centres.

Five Green Areas have been created, running north-south to separate the major cities. In 30 years 27 million trees were planted to try and improve the environment.

Five Area Parks have also been built, close to large towns. These Area Parks are from 25 to 100 hectares in size and include swimming pools, solariums, fitness centres and team game facilities. Usually 25-50,000 people live within 15 minutes' walking time of each Area Park.

Leisure Areas cover up to 300 hectares, including a minimum of 60

Below **Substantial green spaces are clearly visible on this map of the Ruhr. The area is also well provided with leisure areas.**

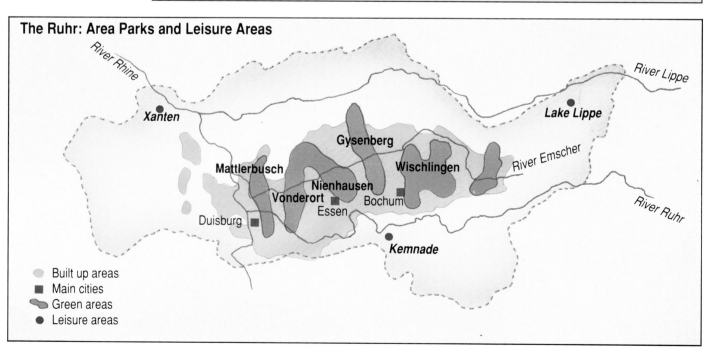

The Ruhr: Area Parks and Leisure Areas

River Rhine
River Lippe
Xanten
Lake Lippe
Gysenberg
Mattlerbusch
Wischlingen
River Emscher
Nienhausen
Vonderort
Bochum
Duisburg
Essen
River Ruhr
Kemnade

- Built up areas
- Main cities
- Green areas
- Leisure areas

hectares of water, to cater for the interest in water sports in these areas. Leisure Zones are smaller versions of Leisure Areas, covering only 150 hectares but still including water areas. Leisure Centres are only 10-25 hectares in size and cater for people in small towns, who are further from the larger Leisure Areas.

In these ways the Ruhr area has been opened up to create many more attractive green spaces for leisure activities.

Lelystad – a Dutch new town

Lelystad has been built on land reclaimed from the sea. Such land is called a polder, and Lelystad is the capital of one huge polder. The town was built to take people who were forced to move out of Amsterdam as older, slum housing was demolished. Lelystad was also designed to provide jobs, so that people would not need to commute to Amsterdam.

The first houses were built in 1967 and by 1990 the population of Lelystad was 44,300. The town is built as four neighbourhood units clustered around a central area. Each neighbourhood unit is traffic free and centred around a primary school. Eighty per cent of homes are single family houses with garages and small gardens. Blocks of flats proved not so popular. Despite careful planning, there are not enough local jobs, so people still commute to Amsterdam.

Solntsevo – Russia

Solntsevo is about 30 km south-west of Moscow. In the 1960s the planners decided to develop the site to take overspill population from Moscow. The capital city could not expand fast enough to take all the new arrivals from the countryside, and so Solntsevo was built. The town was planned in the mikroraion (neighbourhood unit) idea, similar to that used in Lelystad. Each mikroraion has its traffic-free housing areas, together with central shops, schools and recreational facilities. By 1990 Solntsevo's population had grown to 67,500. However there are still problems:–

• There are not enough shops in the mikroraions.

• Many people still have to commute to Moscow because there are not enough jobs in Solntsevo.

• Some of the blocks of flats suffer from damp because they were built in a hurry.

• There is a lack of public services such as libraries, schools and cinemas.

At one time, many people thought new towns would solve most of Europe's urban problems. They have solved some difficulties, but in the process have created others.

a new town is to choose a green field site, and then carefully plan the layout of the whole town to ensure the best use of the space. In this way, for example, industry

This map illustrates the Russian 'mikroraion' plan. The area is completely self-contained, and all essential services are easily accessible.

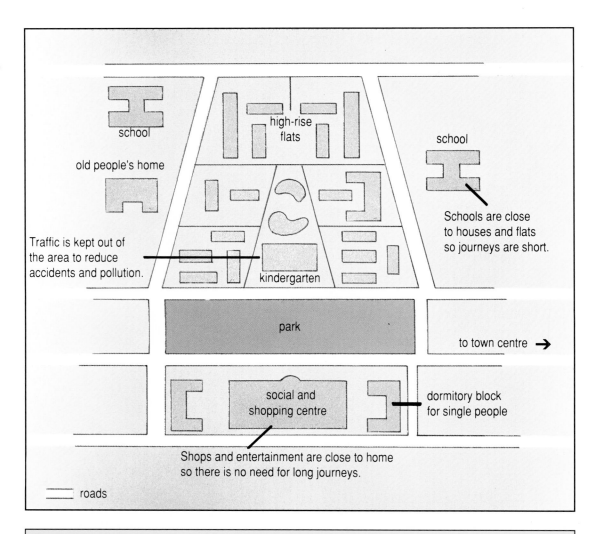

school

high-rise flats

old people's home

school

Schools are close to houses and flats so journeys are short.

Traffic is kept out of the area to reduce accidents and pollution.

kindergarten

park

to town centre →

social and shopping centre

dormitory block for single people

Shops and entertainment are close to home so there is no need for long journeys.

roads

Urban sprawl – the case of the Netherlands

In the western part of the Netherlands a group of towns close together have grown and spread over large areas of countryside. The maps show how these towns have expanded since 1900. The whole area is now called 'Randstad' which means 'The Ringed City'. It is a horseshoe shape of towns, stretching from Dordrecht and Rotterdam, to Delft, The Hague, Amsterdam and Utrecht. Since 1900 the population there has increased from 1 million to 6.5 million in 1990. As the towns grow, they are joining together to form one large built-up area, called a conurbation. Very little open space is left between the towns. Recently the Dutch planners have tried to ensure that an area of open space

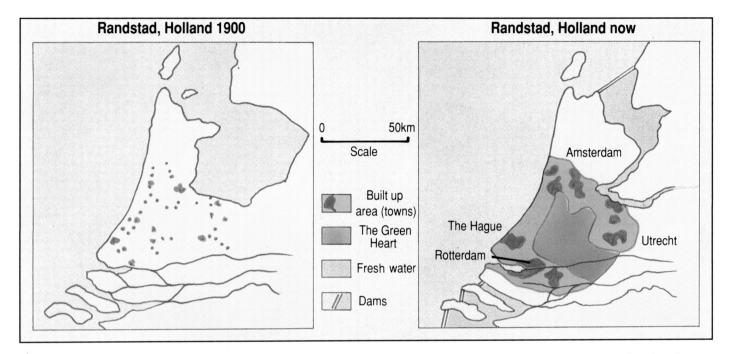

Randstad, Holland 1900

Randstad, Holland now

Scale
0 — 50km

Built up area (towns)

The Green Heart

Fresh water

Dams

Amsterdam

The Hague

Rotterdam

Utrecht

Map showing the urban sprawl over the course of the twentieth century in the Randstad area of the Netherlands. The urban centres are spreading and gradually merging.

and agricultural land is preserved as the 'green heart' of the Randstad. The idea is to prevent further urban development in this central, green area.

As the Randstad has grown, several major problems have emerged. There is the need to build many new housing estates to cope with the increase in population. The Randstad only covers 16 per cent of the whole Netherlands area, but it houses 42 per cent of the nation's people. New motorways and underground railways are also needed to connect the different parts of Randstad.

The movement of people out to the edges of the Randstad towns is another problem. Between 1970 and 1980 the central parts of Rotterdam lost 17 per cent of their population to the suburbs. The figure for Amsterdam is 15 per cent and for The Hague is 18 per cent.

Another problem is loss of land. Industry is growing and taking an extra 5,000 hectares of land each year, while more land has been lost as the airport at Schipol has been expanded. Air and water pollution are serious problems because people and industry are confined to a small area.

Now the Dutch are planning the Randstad area as a whole, in order to improve the quality of life for its people.

can be located away from houses and flats, and enough green space can be provided. Two examples, one from the Netherlands and one from Russia, show how new towns work in practice.

Ethnic minorities in Samarkand

Ethnic minorities moved to some cities in the CIS in search of work. In other cases, such as in Samarkand, the ethnic minority is the local people. They were conquered in the past when the area became part of the Soviet Union.

About 338,000 people live in Samarkand now, but it is still possible to recognize three different parts of the city, all of which contain different mixtures of ethnic groups.

Near the city centre is the traditional quarter. This is very like many other Muslim cities with narrow, winding streets, flat-roofed houses and the minarets (towers) of local mosques. In this area live the local Uzbek people.

Further away from the city centre is the area called the Russian New Town.

This is an area of straight, wide streets, lined with shady trees and blocks of flats. This zone was built in the eighteenth century after the Russians conquered the town. Now the main ethnic group in this part of town are the Russians themselves.

Beyond the Russian New Town is the part of Samarkand built after 1917 (the year of the Russian Revolution). This is an area of tower blocks of flats that has a population of both Uzbeks and Russians.

Usually people from different ethnic groups live in harmony in Europe's cities. However, problems do still arise. Ethnic minorities often live in poorer housing and have a lower income than other local people. There can be hostility between people from different ethnic groups who may face discrimination in some cities.

It is clear from this map of Samarkand that the traditional centre has developed haphazardly, whereas the straight streets of the Russian and Soviet sectors have been planned and laid out.

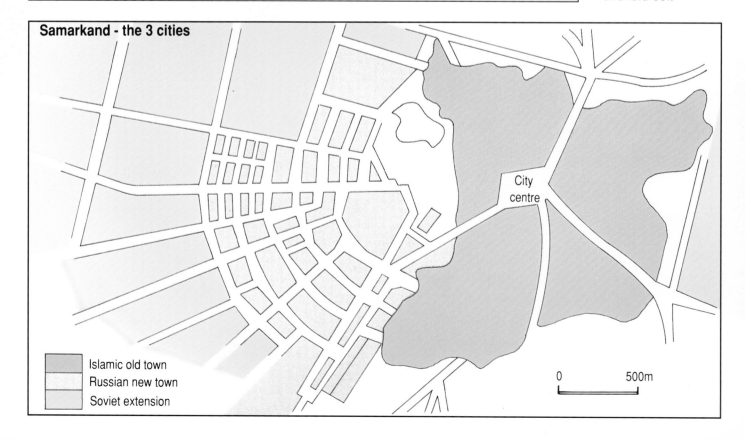

Samarkand - the 3 cities

City centre

Islamic old town
Russian new town
Soviet extension

0   500m

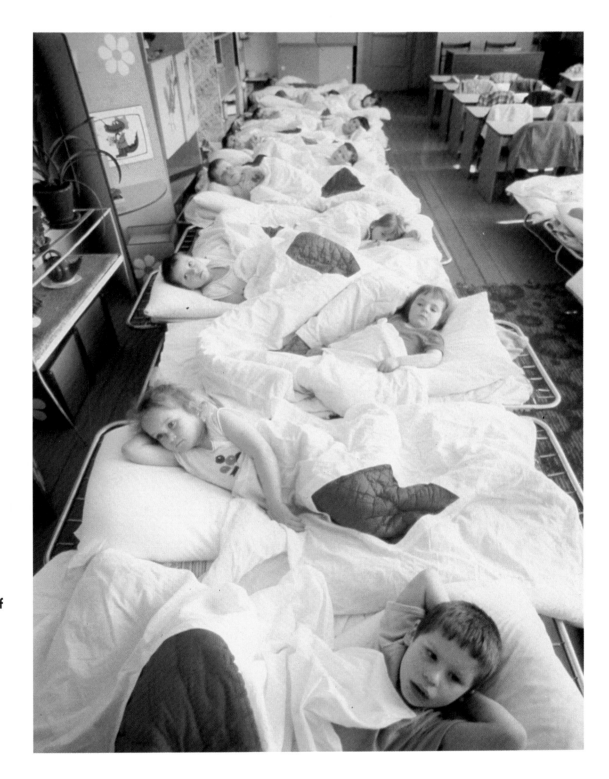

The consequences of the nuclear reactor meltdown at Chernobyl are still being felt today. These local children are in hospital, suffering intestinal problems brought about by exposure to the radiation.

Negative factors include:
- Stress, related to a rapid pace of life. This can lead to high rates of crime, alcoholism and suicide.
- A poor physical environment, illustrated by polluted rivers and lakes, derelict land and high levels of air pollution.
- Unemployment, high rates of which represent a waste of human potential, as well as causing extreme financial hardship.

Variations in Europe

Taking both positive and negative factors into consideration, geographers have produced a map which shows how the quality of life varies from one country to another in Europe. The map shows quite sharp differences between European countries. Sweden emerges as the country with the highest quality of life, followed by Germany. Beyond this are a group of countries with quite a high quality of life, namely Switzerland, Belgium, the United Kingdom, Denmark, France, the Netherlands and Norway. It is the nations on the southern and western edge of Europe which seem to have the poorest quality of life. These are Greece, Spain, Portugal and Ireland.

However it is important to remember points about these maps:
- If different indicators of the

quality of life had been chosen, a different map would have resulted.
- Important differences occur *within* the countries and these are not shown on this map. For example, in Germany there are big differences between life in the decaying, polluted regions, like parts of the Ruhr, and the attractive, expanding areas of the Black Forest.

Index of quality of life

Best

↓

Worst

Above **Map showing how the quality of life varies between different European countries.**

Top right **Closely packed blocks of flats at Cluj in Romania.**

Right **This chart shows the pattern of holiday-taking and holiday-expenditure throughout Europe.**

Percentage of families who take a holiday each year (1989)

Sweden	68%
U.K.	64%
Germany	61%
Denmark	59%
Norway	57%
France	54%
The Netherlands	54%
Belgium	52%
Italy	50%
Spain	45%
Portugal	40%

Which countries spend most on their holidays?

Germany (West)	27.1
U.K.	17.0
Spain	15.3
Italy	15.1
France	12.4
Holland	5.1
Belgium	4.2
Denmark	4.1
Sweden	3.7
Norway	2.9
Portugal	1.1

In £ billion

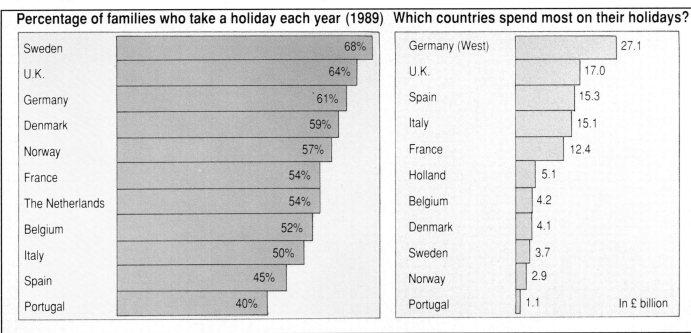

The future for Europe

The pattern of quality of life is constantly changing and may well look very different in thirty years' time. Some areas may become prosperous, for example, through the development of new resources or the growth of new industries. Other regions could decay and the quality of life may fall as unemployment rises. Increasingly, the European Community (EC) makes vigorous efforts to ensure that people in all its regions have a roughly comparable quality of life. The main instrument of this work is the Regional Fund, which offers grants and loans to encourage development projects in areas with a lower quality of life. Schemes such as new or improved roads, new factories and trading estates, and even help to improve the environment, are part of the work of the Regional Fund.

Parks and green spaces within cities, such as Kensington Gardens in London, provide leisure and sporting facilities and greatly enhance the citizens' quality of life.

Opposite page **This map shows the formation of the EC.**

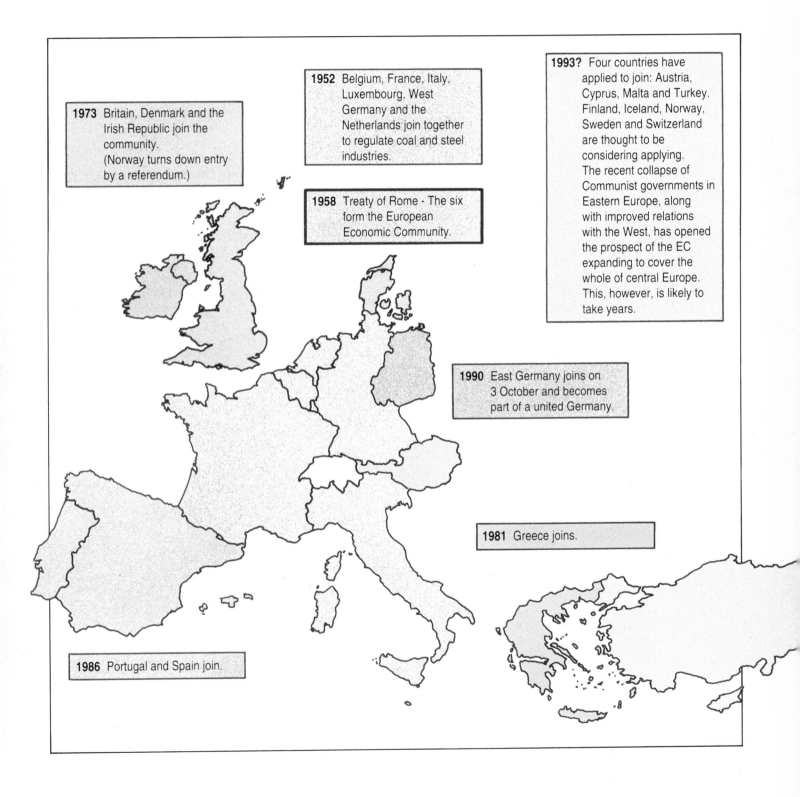

1973 Britain, Denmark and the Irish Republic join the community. (Norway turns down entry by a referendum.)

1952 Belgium, France, Italy, Luxembourg, West Germany and the Netherlands join together to regulate coal and steel industries.

1958 Treaty of Rome - The six form the European Economic Community.

1993? Four countries have applied to join: Austria, Cyprus, Malta and Turkey. Finland, Iceland, Norway, Sweden and Switzerland are thought to be considering applying. The recent collapse of Communist governments in Eastern Europe, along with improved relations with the West, has opened the prospect of the EC expanding to cover the whole of central Europe. This, however, is likely to take years.

1990 East Germany joins on 3 October and becomes part of a united Germany.

1981 Greece joins.

1986 Portugal and Spain join.

Glossary

COMMUTE To travel some distance to and from work.

CONGESTION A concentration of traffic or a traffic jam.

CONSERVED Protected for the future.

DERELICT No longer maintained by people. This results in buildings falling into disrepair and land becoming overgrown.

DEVELOPMENT PLAN A plan which aims to make the best use of the land.

DROUGHT A long period without rainfall, causing a water shortage.

ENVIRONMENT All our surroundings, whether natural (such as plants, rivers, cliffs) or artificial (such as buildings, factories, motorways).

IMMIGRANTS People who move from one country to live in another.

IRRIGATION Supplying water to farmland using artificial canals or a sprinkling system.

LAND USE The purpose for which land is used

LIFESTYLE The way people live their lives.

MULTI-PURPOSE Designed for several uses.

NATIONAL PARK A large, mainly rural area which has outstanding natural scenery and wildlife – protected for public enjoyment.

NEW TOWN A planned settlement with its own industry, housing, leisure and shopping facilities.

OUTSKIRTS The outer parts of a town.

POLLUTION The presence in the environment of harmful substances, such as smoke from factory chimneys or dangerous chemical waste.

REDEVELOPMENT Attempts to rebuild and improve an area.

RURAL Of the countryside.

SLAG HEAP A large mound of waste material from coal mining or steel making processes.

SUBURB A housing area on the outskirts of a town or city.

URBAN FRINGE The area of houses and countryside at the edge of a town or city.

Books to read

Crossley, Steve: People in the Urban Landscape (Macdonald, 1987).

Flint, David: Economic Geography (Longman, 1990).

Foskett, Rosalind and Nicholas: People in the Rural Landscape (Macdonald, 1987).

Gillett, Jack: Urban and Rural Geography (Longman, 1988).

Groushko, M. (ed): The Mediterranean Environment (Chanceral, 1985).

Haigh, Michael: Around Britain and Europe (C.U.P., 1985).

Martin, Fred and Whittle, Aubrey: Cities (Hutchinson, 1986).

Martin, Fred and Whittle, Aubrey: Leisure (Hutchinson, 1986).

Minshall, Gordon: Western Europe (Hodder and Stoughton, 1989).

Penny, Malcolm: Pollution and Conservation (Wayland, 1988).

Pracht, Louis (ed): Europe in Figures (Macmillan, 1989).

Prowse, Duncan: The Mountain Environment (Chanceral, 1980).

Punnett, Neil: Western Europe (Basil Blackwell, 1987).

Waugh, David: Europe (Nelson, 1985).

Further information

You can contact these organizations to find out more about the issues covered in this book.

C.E.A.T. (Coordination Europenne des Amis de la Terre)
Rue Blanche 29
1050 Brussels
Belgium

Commission of the European Communities
8 Storey's Gate
London
SW1P 3AT

Council of Europe
Boîte Postale 431 R6
67006 Strasbourg Cedex
France

Earthscan
3, Endsleigh Street
London WC1H 0DD and 1717,
Massachusetts Avenue
Washington DC 20036 USA

Europeo,
Henk Meyer, IDG
Geographical Institute
State University
Heidelberglaan 2
P.O. Box 80115
3508 TC, Utrecht
Netherlands

Eurostat
Statistical Office of the European Communities
L 2920 Luxembourg

UNESCO
7 Place de Fontenoy
Paris
France

Index